Project Management

A Beginner's Guide To Effectively Manage Any Project Like The Pros Do

By Adam Richards

Table of Contents

Introduction

What This Book Is About

In Chapter 1, you will learn what project management actually is and the required various groups of activities that carry a project from start to finish. You will also find out the features a project has to have, in order to be considered as successful and of course the common constraints of project management.

In the next chapter, we will discuss a little more about the primary 3 constraints (time, cost, scope) and the use of the Iron Triangle (also known as project management triangle). Furthermore, you will also learn about the Euler Diagram (also known as "Pick Any Two" diagram).

Planning is crucial and Chapter 3 is solely dedicated to this phase of project management. We will first go through the problems that might come across, if you do not have a solid plan for your project and then we will go through each of the required steps you need to take, that will help you design an effective management plan.

Meeting deadlines is of the essence if you want to be successful at managing a project of any kind and in the same time, it can be quite frustrating if you don't. In the next chapter, you will learn what is needed of you to make sure that you meet your deadlines.

Problems will always come along the way; some maybe minor while others can be devastating. Therefore, developing a solution oriented mindset will help you deal with such obstacles while finding a way around them. In Chapter 5, you will learn the qualities a good project manager has to have and how to tackle any probable or improbable project hindrances.

Furthermore, we will discuss about Risks and how you can handle them effectively, the things you have to do when you actually miss a deadline and what happens if an unexpected project crops up. In addition, you will learn in detail about Issues and how they should be managed, so you can increase the chances of completing your project promptly.

Finally, in the last chapter you will learn how to make a proper evaluation of your overall performance by reviewing project activities, interviewing team members or surveying with questionnaires. Furthermore, you will find out about reporting and the features a final project report needs to have.

On top of that, you will also find out 13 more project management tips that I strongly believe will be helpful to you in order to have a successful project.

Once again, thank you for purchasing this book, I hope you enjoy it!

Chapter 1:

Project Management 101

What Is Project Management?

I am sure you have come across the term "project management" quite often in class or in the professional sphere. However, do you know exactly what project management means?

A very simple definition of a Project is;

A project is a series of well-planned tasks, which you undertake keeping in mind various limitations such as time, resources and the desired result.

The word *project* is derived from the Latin word *"projectum"*. The word *"projectum"* comes from the Latin verb *"proicere"*. In this word "pro" means "before" and the word *"iacere"*, means, "to do". Thus, the word "project" leads to the connotation "before an action".

With that being said, ***Project Management*** refers to the process of implementing knowledge both functional and technical, skills and techniques in day-to-day project activities to manage it effectively and efficiently. In order for you to better understand what project management is, we will look at the different project management activities.

Project Management Activities

Project management activities can be broadly classified into the following groups:

Initiating

Planning

Organizing

Executing

Monitoring and controlling

Motivating

Closing

The goal of project management is to devise various procedures for these areas in project execution in order to streamline the path to achieve project objectives or goals.

The importance of project management in the present times cannot be ignored. Whether you are managing an academic project or a professional project, displaying of good managerial skill set will put you way ahead of others in the rat race.

Project management offers a great deal of learning and helps build an overall knowledge of every aspect of business. If you are adept at managing projects skillfully, it is likely to increase your chances of being a good leader.

Project management is important, as you need to know the skills that you need to manage a project effectively to ensure that it is a success, which brings us to the other important thing; what exactly is a successful project. For a project to be considered successful, it has to be backed with the following features:

A Convincing Idea

A plausible and a convincing idea is the pre-requisite of a successful project. Get a judicious validation of the idea to ensure that it doesn't disappoint you at a later stage when it fails. The idea should be established after extensive research before it becomes the foundation of a project.

Clear Goals

Any project, however ambitious, is likely to go haywire if it is not backed up with clear goals. In any case, how will you know if the project is successful if you do not know how to measure its success.

Once you have clear goals, you will have an easier time managing the project, as your plans will revolve around clear goals.

Adequate planning

We all know that failing to plan is planning to fail. You will know the success of a project depending on the amount of planning that has been put into it.

Practical Project milestones

In the absence of practical and reasonable milestones, a project is likely to lose its steam and unlikely to meet the set deadlines. This would further help in making the project financially viable.

Back-up Plan

Keeping in mind the risk factor and chances of professional jeopardy, keep a flexible and a sensible back-up plan.

Team Cohesiveness

There is no denial in the fact that a reliable and a well-knit team is an asset. Such a team is effective in executing a project successfully and realizing its winning closure.

Stays within the Budget

Every project will surely have a budget. A successful project is one that stays within the budget.

Completed on time

As you start a project, you will have set time limits and deadlines that you have to adhere to. If a project is completed within the required time, then for sure it is a success with respect to the time requirements.

Common Constraints Of Project Management

Project management is all about working towards the pertinent goals while respecting the various constraints imposed upon a project. Constraints may be self-imposed or natural. The primary constraints are:

Scope

Refers to the planned deliverables and the mode of achieving them.

Timeframe

Set or proposed time to reach different milestones in any project until completion.

Budget allocation

Finances and other resources like labor, raw material and equipment.

Quality

The desired quality of the job or the primary goal of the project.

Resources

Procure and allocate resources at various points in orderly fashion keeping in mind the budget and smooth running of project.

Chapter 2:

How To Effectively Manage Your Project While Keeping In Mind These 3 Key Constraints

As stated in the previous chapter, a project is governed by constraints. Constraints are present in any and every practical system.

A project, which tries to achieve some goal, will also have certain constraints. Project management is about dealing with constraints involved optimally.

Constraints should not be a roadblock in path of effective decision making for a successful project execution, completion and management. You can manage a project using different models; we will discuss some of these models in this chapter.

Iron Triangle

To get visualization of challenges and difficulties arising while executing a project, a visualization aid called *iron triangle* is used. This is also known as *project management triangle*. It is used to access the constraints in advance before a project is implemented for better decision making at the time of execution.

The Iron Triangle

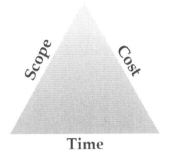

Iron triangle or a project management triangle deals with three primary constraints involved in a project. However, there may be other interdependent constraints depending on the size of the project.

The three primary interdependent constraints shown in triangle are

Time involved

Cost involved

Scope of project

The center of the triangle lays quality, which is the primary goal of a project activity. The entire structure can be improved a step further if quality is not considered a goal but, constraint. It will be added as another dimension (or side) but the triangle will then become a pyramid.

The basic principle behind the triangle model is that, since constraints are interdependent, changing one will affect the other two. Like in a triangle if you change the length of one side, you will definitely affect the whole triangle including the other two sides.

In order to understand how these constraints affect project management, let's discuss each of these constraints in detail:

Scope

This looks at the outcome of the project. It defines the list of deliverables of the project and the path to achieve this. Change in any point of scope will affect others.

Generally, increased scope means increase in time allocation and cost of project.

Time

Amount of time allocated to complete the project can be split for each individual task for better monitoring and control. Time taken will depend on factors like amount of resources involved, experience or exposure to work and skill set of individuals among other things.

Tight time constraint usually means increased cost and reduced scope.

Cost

It is always important for the management team to take cost consideration before every planned step involved in a project. Budget and cost allocation will determine the amount of resources dedicated to each task and will have adverse effects on the timelines and scope. A tight or stringent cost allocation could drastically reduce the amount of resources involved, drag timelines and reduce scope.

"Pick Any Two" Euler Diagram

We can visualize the complexity that is present in a project with the help of the above Iron Triangle. However, there are usually unlimited possibilities in the plane bounded by any three constraints. In order for us to consider these possibilities, we have to consider a better form of project triangle.

The Euler diagram also known as "pick any two" is thus helpful in these situations. The Euler diagram has three sides of triangle, which are denoted with three circular structures.

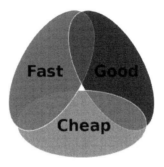

The three circular structures represent *Fast*, *Good* and *Cheap* and they intersect each other at points to represent a triangle. *Fast* refers to delivery time or schedule, *good* defines quality and *Cheap* represents the cost of designing and building a product.

This diagram connotes the ideology that 'no matter what, it is never possible to optimize all constraints. One will always lag'.

Cost cannot be minimized if high quality product is to be delivered within a short span of time.

Product will not be of high quality if time is reduced along with cost.

To deliver high quality products at a cheaper cost you tend to take lot of time.

Chapter 3:

How To Design A Simple, Practical And Easy To Follow Plan For Your Project

Planning is very important before starting any project. Planning is critical as it helps us carry out the tasks involved in the project in an organized manner, ruling out the unnecessary confusion that we might come across during the course of the project.

Before we learn the various steps involved in planning, it is imperative for us to know what might be the probable problems if we don't have an adequate plan for the execution of our project.

Fail to meet the project deadline

Due to lack of planning, it might not be possible for us to complete the project within the stipulated time. This would have consequent and cascading effects on other aspects of project.

Be in a Mess

You might just end up in a big mess. Instead of smooth execution, your project might be the reason for your sleepless nights.

So, think ahead but do not anticipate senselessly.

Affect the relationship with client

If your client is unhappy with the way you work, this might affect your relationship in future. Furthermore, they are unlikely to give you any work if you are unable to finish tasks on time.

Degradation of performance

Your performance will definitely go down thus affecting your overall performance, incentive or promotion.

Adverse effect on business

The Business is likely to be affected adversely if projects are not executed in a systematic way. The lack of planning and management will take a toll on the business and its associated activities.

However, with the right planning, any sort of challenge in project management can be dealt with smartly.

How To Design An Effective Management Plan

Designing an effective management plan is no easy task. It requires time, effort and money; however, when you are done with the process, you will be glad that you did it. In order to have an effective management plan, you will need to follow some important steps. We will have a look at these steps and the details of each one of them.

Set a goal

If you know what exactly you want to accomplish and you are able to portray the same to your team members, almost 60 per cent of the work is done. The concept should be well-defined and vivid to you members as well. Ensure that you set SMART goals. This simply means that your goal or rather goals should be specific, measurable, achievable, realistic and have time constraints.

Allocation of Resources

Determination of the right amount of resources according to the work requirement is mandatory for successful project execution. After deciding on the resources, assigning each one of these resources the specific work is important. If it is labor, you need to assign tasks accordingly to ensure that the project is completed within the set time limit. Work distribution if done in a proper way can do wonders.

Creation of requirement list

Talk to each of your clients for their specific needs and requirements to accomplish the assigned tasks and accordingly prepare a requirement list so that you are fully equipped right from the beginning of the project.

Come up with an action plan

Depending on the timeframe, your action plan should be clear so as to accomplish the tasks sequentially. You should be in a position to visualize the entire path leading to the completion of the project.

Identification of risk factors

You should be aware of the probable risk areas, assess them and take measures to keep the risks minimized. This will ensure that nothing gets you unaware in the course of the project implementation.

Creation of a backup system

A backup system should be created before beginning a project as a preventive measure from losing any important data in case of professional crisis or jeopardy. This will ensure that not only will your data remain secure but will also ensure uninterrupted execution of the project during the emergency.

Effective communication with all stakeholders

Everyone should be aware of the objectives, benefits and their individual involvement in the project.

Chapter 4:

How To Meet Your Deadlines And Make Sure The Work Gets Done

Meeting deadlines can be frustrating at times especially when a lot needs to be done with a short timeframe. While you would need to stick to tight schedules, delivering quality work is also crucial. So, how do you meet deadlines for whatever project effectively?

We will look at what you actually need to do to ensure that you meet your deadlines.

Start with a plan

Planning is the key to meeting project deadlines. Even though planning might cost you some time, it is worth every minute. In any case, how would you know your final destination if you do not make the necessary plans?

You should be aware of the steps that would lead to your final destination.

You would also have to do all the brainstorming required to accomplish the task sequentially. How you plan to achieve your goals should be clear right from the beginning.

Actually, it is advisable that you pen-down your to-do list for clarity of thoughts.

Estimate time

Now you have a plan, what next. You need to determine the period within which you will undertake the project using the established plan. Suppose the actual project deadline is in the sixth month, then the estimated deadline should be in the fifth month itself.

You should be done with all pertaining processes so that you can utilize the remaining time to revise the plan, see if you have followed to what you wanted to achieve and make the necessary changes.

The only way that you can estimate the total time for project completion is through estimating the timeframe for each individual task then you add up the time involved.

Keep track of progress

You may have an amazing plan as well as have the expected timeframe for the project. However, you will only adhere to these if you can track your progress appropriately. Internal deadlines also referred to as milestones for the completion of each task by every team member help in monitoring the progress of the project.

Interaction on a daily basis with the stakeholders makes you aware of the issues they are facing and helps in keeping track of work progress. This also helps you in solving the issues as they crop up and sometimes even before they strike.

Manage resources effectively

The team members should never feel the lack of necessary resources to accomplish the project. Your goal is to ensure that members have access to the required resources and if there are any constraints, you improvise.

You should also ensure that the team members are aware of the constraints so that they can use the available resources accordingly to accomplish the assigned task.

Deal with problems

Sometimes things don't fall in place irrespective of all the prior planning. This kind of situation might crop up anytime.

The wisest thing for you to do is to identify the problem, assess its root cause and come up with possible solutions. The sooner it is done, the better it is for meeting the project deadline.

Be focused and determined

A focused leader will definitely inspire the team. Inspiration can work wonders. Do you know that your team members will simply go the extra mile with a little bit of inspiration?

This is why it is of utmost importance to be inspired so that you can inspire your team members.

Have a Positive attitude

Optimism is a vital attribute of every individual. It gives you an edge, and in any case at the end of the day, attitude matters. As a beginner, you might require some time to inculcate optimism within you but it surely comes along with practice.

If you are a leader and handling a bunch of people, positive attitude is a must. If you believe that the work can be done on time, your attitude will make your team believe too.

Chapter 5:

How To Handle Any Unexpected Problems That Might Come Along The Way

Before we go on to discuss the problems and hindrances that may mar the success of a project, let us first know about all the qualities that you need to develop in you to manage your project productively.

Apart from all the techniques, tools and methodologies, it is important to develop a savvy mindset that would steer you ahead confidently.

Qualities of a Good Project Manager

If you are to handle problems adequately, you need to have some specific qualities. We will look at these qualities so that you know what is expected of you if you want to solve problems.

Be Far-sighted

Develop a sense of foresight so that you can foresee any impending problem. Having a sense of anticipation can save you from situations that you could have easily avoided.

Be a Planner

Be an inherent organizer and do not leave anything

to chance. Being a smart planner and organizer will help you know how to manage the project adequately to avoid impending problems. In any case, planning is likely to reduce the problems you my face by almost 50%.

Be a Leader

Since a project may involve many dimensions and aspects, you as its manager have to be a leader. You may have to interact with teams, vendors, clients, sponsors etc and influence them. This can be effectively done by being a natural and an effortless leader. Your leading stance will act as an innate motivation for your team members.

Be a good Communicator

Communication would be your key to successfully handling the project. Make ample use of your communication skills and other aids like meetings, e-mails, video conferencing etc to resolve the issues and to meet targets optimally. Saying and conveying what you want to convey would be a great way to ensure that the set goals and objectives are met.

Be Practical

Although it is good to want everything to be perfect, you need to be practical about it. If you are a perfectionist, you are likely to expect too much from other team members such that you may end up affecting their ability to deliver results leading to frustrations and disappointments. Always be a practical leader if you want to avoid unnecessary problems.

Be Considerate

Being considerate and empathetic will enable you to understand others' point of view. This would in turn enable you to understand the scenario such that you can start tackling it.

Tackling Probable and Improbable Project Hindrances

Problems can crop up any time in the life cycle of a project. In fact, while handling a project, unexpected problems and questions almost always come along the way. Therefore, you should be ready and equipped to deal with such issues or else they can potentially affect the progress of your project and the outcome as well.

If you don't want to see your failure, expecting the unexpected is the wisest way out. You may have developed all the appropriate plans for the project and think that everything has been put into consideration; however, you don't want to be too confident such that you overlook some things. Always know that your action plan might give rise to unexpected problems that you must be prepared to handle and resolve.

One of the most effective ways of dealing with project problems is identifying the root causes of the problem and resolving them. Such issues can then be resolved quickly and effectively without affecting the project progress adversely. Project risk management and issue management almost resemble with only slight variation.

Issues Vs Risks

The exact nature of both issues and risks remains largely unknown. We tend to have a general idea about risks in advance and keep a partial or a complete back-up plan. On the other hand, issues are less predictable, they may arise without any prior warning.

For instance, inability to find the apt human resource for a specific task is an identifiable risk. However, when one of your human resources falls sick for a couple of weeks, it becomes an issue.

Estimation and identification of risks prior to

working on the project is extremely important, as it can help you with prioritizing the risk areas and creating an action plan to combat them proactively. However, issues can't be estimated in advance, which means that they require instant resolution as and when they arise.

Issue management is a planned process that helps us to deal with any sort of unexpected problem arising during the course of the project at its earliest. Lets first understand how you can handle risks effectively before moving on to discuss about how to manage issues.

How To Handle Risks

#1 Set realistic goals

Setting an ambitious goal of executing a certain project within a miraculously short time is recipe for disappointment since reality is always far from perfect. Therefore, it is paramount that you set realistic goals and deadlines if you are to avoid the risk of not fulfilling what you have planned to achieve.

#2 Plan for the unexpected

Although project delays could be expected, the timing, probability, the nature and the impact is often unexpected. So, instead of just assuming that everything will be fine, it is always important to have a clear plan of how to deal with all unexpected occurrences.

#3 Have a risk minimization plan that entails:

Being aware of everything that is happening in the project so that you can tell the warning sign of things to come

Proper scheduling that factors in any probable delays even when the probability is unknown.

Proper communication of the status of a project is a good way of managing expectations for everyone. This minimizes disappointments and other unexpected conflicts.

Follow a specific process so that everyone understands where you are as far as the project is

concerned.

After having all these plans in place, what do you do when you actually miss a project deadline?

#1

Learn to accept the missed deadline and communicate to stakeholders: People will be more forgiving if you inform them about project delays before they ask about it; don't just keep quiet.

#2

Get the necessary resources in place and figure out how you can actually mitigate the problem.

#3

Consider and communicate the consequences: After missing the deadline, you need to highlight the cost of missing the deadline and remind the stakeholders of how they would "benefit" even after the delay. The situation must be a win-win for everyone.

So, what happens if an unexpected project crops up?

#1

Learn the art of crashing: In this case, you need to bring in more staff and other resources to ensure that you complete the project promptly.

#2

Fast track by combining some of the steps or phases of the project for faster completion. For example, it could entail combining the design stage with the build stage in a project.

#3

Use the constrained resource scheduling technique, which entails using strategies that have worked in the past for a current project. This means that some of the steps need to be skipped or at best refined.

#4

You can as well change some of the expectations or deliverables of some other projects so that you can squeeze in the current project. This means stretching the current resources to their limit so that they can handle the expanded project scope.

How To Manage Issues

Issues are some of the greatest contributors of different project risks. Let's first understand how you can manage issues as they arise so that you can increase the chances of completing any project promptly.

We will discuss the issue management process in detail for a clear picture:

Issues should be logged or recorded as and when they crop up. They should be reported and communicated at a level where you are answerable to. This can help you with some beneficial inputs on dealing with the unexpected problem and resolving it quickly and effectively. It also ensures that issues are thoroughly investigated to avoid unnecessary trouble in future. Having a lenient attitude towards issues can worsen the situation and it might be too late to troubleshoot them.

Before logging an issue, you should be aware of the content in an issue log. You may include the following in an issue log:

Type of issues

You are likely to encounter different types of issues when managing any project. Defining an issue in a particular category is important for assigning the right person to resolve them.

The possible categories are:

Technical
Resource
Change in business strategies
Change in management
Third party

Identifier

The name of the person who actually discovered the issue should be recorded. This would help in getting the first version of the snag or the issue encountered.

Timing

The timing of identifying the issue should be logged as well to gauge its enormity.

Description

Details of what happened and the potential impact should be an integral part of issue log for better understanding and effective resolving.

Priority

Priority rating should be assigned to the issue for future reference and project learning. An issue can either be high priority, medium priority or low priority depending on its impact on project progress and success.

Assignment of a responsible person

The person responsible for resolving the issue should be determined based on the issue type.

Target resolution date

A deadline should be set for resolving the issue depending on the priority level.

Status

The progress of the issue resolution can be found out by tracking it on a timely basis. Thus, defining an overall status to the issue is the smartest way to figure out the current scenario. Status can either be open, investigating, implementing, escalated or resolved.

This gives a clear understanding about the amount of attention and time required to resolve the issue.

Action/resolution description

The resolution of the issue if already done, should be recorded in a chronological order.

Final resolution

A summary of all the actions taken to address the issue can be recorded in this space.

The issue logs can be of great help in terms of emergency. If similar issue persists someday, it can be dealt with in an orderly manner without investing much time in investigating the causes and finding the right people for resolution of the issue. The specific areas of strength of every individual can be determined from the issue log.

Once issue log is done, supplementing an issue management framework is the next thing to do. Framework depicts the actual process for dealing with the issue.

It gives a clear understanding to the project team regarding the responsibilities to be performed. The framework also provides a structure that helps in quick and effective decision making when issues arise.

Both issue logs and issue management framework capture lessons that can be referred for future projects. They make you fully equipped and prepared for any subsequent issues or problems somewhat related to the previously logged issues.

Even if the future problems are not connected to the logged issues, they ensure a practical knowledge that can undoubtedly be of great help in resolving issues that you might come along in your next project.

Chapter 6:

How To End Your Project And Evaluate Your Overall Performance

After tedious execution of a project, its winding remains to be accomplished which is equally a daunting task. After all the hard work and effort that have been put in to reach the end of your project, if the finishing is not adequately executed, it may lead to client dissatisfaction, which is certainly not desirable.

To maintain a long-term goodwill with clients, summation of project in the right way is extremely important. Here are a few points that you should not overlook when you are on the verge of completing of your project.

Evaluation

When you are almost done with a project, this is the time when you should gather your team for a comprehensive assessment of your project. Assessment is necessary to determine whether your project has fulfilled its aims and objectives or not.

Evaluation can also provide a fuller picture to the stakeholders who have rendered either financial or technical support to the project. It also acts as a food for thought for the leading organization to assess the way it has implemented the project and the areas it has gone wrong so that it can design a better project in future. If there are areas for quick improvement, team members can work on those areas for a successful completion of the project. Evaluation also helps in determining if the project has been able to meet the target deadline.

How can you evaluate your project? We will look at the different ways that you can manage the project.

#1 Reviewing project activities

The sequential completion of each task involved in the project can be reviewed for one last time to ensure everything was done properly and nothing went wrong anywhere. A conclusion can be drawn if the team members were successful in completing the project on time and the allocated budget was sufficient to meet all the requirements of the project. If there were issues or hurdles that were along the way of project completion, you need to know how they were dealt with and if they affected the project at large.

#2 Interviewing team members

This involves talking to each team member involved in the project. This helps to assess their level of satisfaction, the hardships they overcame for a successful completion of the project, the impact of the project in their life, their ideas to wind up the project in a better way and their ideas to develop the project further or design new projects in the future.

This can strengthen the relationship between you and your team members. You can record and present these interviews to your client for demonstrating your success. This can be a unique way to end your project with a practical and personalized touch.

#3 Surveying with questionnaires

If you wish to keep a track record of the entire project related events and activities, you can ask each team member to fill up the questionnaires. Based on the data generated, graphs and charts can be prepared for an easy understanding of the project completion. Such dataset can also be used for preparing final project report.

Reporting

A report includes detailed information that present a clear overview of all the aspects of the project. Reports are mainly prepared for clients so that they can understand how the project shaped up and how exactly the targets were achieved. Reports are also presented in front of stakeholders to ensure transparency in business. Proper reporting is indispensable for an easy understanding. In order to make sure that your report can communicate the appropriate information, it needs to have the following features.

#1 Clarity

The first desirable quality in a report is clarity. Your report should not be complicated because your purpose is to reach out to your prospect in terms of comprehensive aspects of the project. I would advise that you keep it as simple as possible. Although it is difficult to summarize the entire development of the project, you should be wise enough to choose your information. Your goal should be presenting how exactly you completed the project successfully.

#2 Structure

Reports must have a clear structure for depicting the right information. The project should have a project code, timeframe, members involved in the project, targets set for the specific timeframe and the way the targets were achieved.

#3 Lessons learnt

A good report comprises of a section that is dedicated to critical assessment of the project as a whole. It states what the organization has learnt during the course of project execution and communicates to the clients in what ways the organization can shape further projects on the basis of the lessons learnt.

Besides the factors stated above, acknowledging all the efforts and hard work of your team members is the most vital factor that you should never miss out on. Successful completion of project is nearly impossible without a dedicated and highly qualified team. When the entire team joins hands in working on a particular project, it progressively reaches its end. Therefore, in the end, it is your team that is the backbone of your project's success, and you must give its due credit.

Bonus:

13 More Project Management Tips

I am sure that you now have all the adequate information for managing a project.

However, you can also make use of the following 13 tips if you want to make sure you will have a successful project.

#Tip No1

Set up your own realm and do not get swayed by pre-defined criteria of successful project management. Edify your own priorities and milestone to avoid sudden problems and thus ensure that nothing happens that you had not anticipated.

#Tip No2

Attain a flexible approach for better functionality. A rigid approach as a project manager may not render realistic results.

#Tip No3

When you set up the project criterion in the initial stage, they should be realistic and well documented. Do not keep any intangible criterion to avoid hazy working.

#Tip No4

However pressure-ridden is your situation, do not commit what you can't fathom to accomplish. In a nutshell, be realistic and vouch for only what you can achieve.

#Tip No5

Segregate situations and people from the problems. Invent newer and out-of-box options that bring in gains for the project.

#Tip No6

In case different projects undergo some changes, you need to update your plan to accommodate the changes.

#Tip No7

Do not limit your managerial skills to just scheduling of your project or in breaking down the structure of project tasks. Give your vital consideration to other vital factors like staff, resource estimates, assumptions, target dates, project metrics, and relationship with vendors and subcontractor.

#Tip No8

If you are managing multiple projects at the same time, adopt a dedicated plan template for each project.

#Tip No9

Do not overburden your project with irrelevant documentation.

Instead of mammoth milestones, set up inch-pebbles for your project. Your estimation and managing will be more effective on breaking larger tasks into multiple smaller ones.

#Tip No10

Do not ignore or sideline quality control. The common mistake that is often committed in projecting management is the pushing of quality control to the last, just before the closing of the project, especially in case of deliverable projects. This throws the rework schedule off-balance.

#Tip No11

Foresee your project risks and combat them just as they arise. Mere identification of the impending risk won't be enough. It is equally important to keep a vigilant eye on the relative perils and threats.

#Tip No12

The initial money and time spent to regularize the project may not show instant results. There will be indeed some short-term loss in the productivity. However, benefits will start showing gradually.

#Tip No13

Base your project estimate on the effective time that would include any emergency or unforeseen interruptions.

Conclusion

Project management can be a daunting task, especially if you are a beginner. However, with proper planning and of course massive action, you will be able to speed up the learning process and become a great project manager in a short time as well. Now is the time to apply the things you have learned so far and put everything into action.

I will be more than happy to learn how this book has helped you in some way. If you feel you have learned something or you think it offered you some value, please take a moment to leave an honest review on Amazon. It would help many future readers who will be forever grateful to you. As I will!

To Your Success,
Adam Richards

Made in the USA
Middletown, DE
20 November 2015